OUR SOLAR SYSTEM
EARTH
THE PLANET OF LIFE

by Mari Schuh

Ideas for Parents and Teachers

Pogo Books let children practice reading informational text while introducing them to nonfiction features such as headings, labels, sidebars, maps, and diagrams, as well as a table of contents, glossary, and index.

Carefully leveled text with a strong photo match offers early fluent readers the support they need to succeed.

Before Reading

- "Walk" through the book and point out the various nonfiction features. Ask the student what purpose each feature serves.
- Look at the glossary together. Read and discuss the words.

Read the Book

- Have the child read the book independently.
- Invite him or her to list questions that arise from reading.

After Reading

- Discuss the child's questions. Talk about how he or she might find answers to those questions.
- Prompt the child to think more. Ask: How is Earth similar to other planets in our solar system? How is it different?

Pogo Books are published by Jump!
5357 Penn Avenue South
Minneapolis, MN 55419
www.jumplibrary.com

Library of Congress Cataloging-in-Publication Data is available at www.loc.gov or upon request from the publisher.

ISBN: 979-8-88524-346-9 (hardcover)
ISBN: 979-8-88524-347-6 (paperback)
ISBN: 979-8-88524-348-3 (ebook)

Editor: Jenna Gleisner
Designer: Emma Bersie

Photo Credits: terimma/Shutterstock, cover (background); max dallocco/Shutterstock, cover (Earth); Anton Balazh/Shutterstock, 1; Tanakorn Moolsarn/Shutterstock, 3; 24K-Production/Shutterstock, 4; RugliG/iStock, 5; forplayday/iStock, 6-7; Ali Ender Birer/Shutterstock, 8-9 (Earth); Goinyk Production/Shutterstock, 8-9 (Sun); Roberto Piras/Shutterstock, 10; Lidiane Miotto/Shutterstock, 11; Naeblys/Shutterstock, 12-13 (Earth); Travel4U/Shutterstock, 12-13 (background); Tilpunov Mikhail/Shutterstock, 14-15 (top); Deni_Sugandi/Shutterstock, 14-15 (bottom); johan63/iStock, 16-17; Alican Akcol/Shutterstock, 18; Pressmaster/Shutterstock, 19 (top); Sergey Novikov/Shutterstock, 19 (bottom); Blue Jean Images/Alamy, 20-21; Delbars/Shutterstock, 23.

Printed in the United States of America at Corporate Graphics in North Mankato, Minnesota.

For Paige

TABLE OF CONTENTS

CHAPTER 1

BLUE PLANET

From space, Earth looks like a blue marble. The blue we see is water. It covers most of the **planet**. Earth is the only planet in our **solar system** with liquid water on its surface. Clouds and ice look white.

clouds

Earth has one moon. The Moon is very bright. It is the brightest object in our night sky. The Moon's **gravity** pulls on Earth. It makes Earth's oceans move. This creates **tides**.

All planets **orbit** the Sun. One full orbit is one year. It takes Earth 365 days to orbit the Sun.

TAKE A LOOK!

Earth is the third planet from the Sun. Take a look!

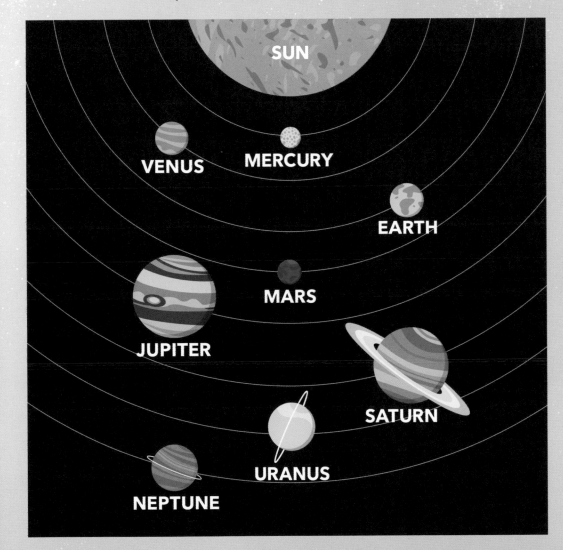

Like all planets, Earth also spins. One full spin is one day. One spin, or Earth day, is 24 hours.

Earth spins on its **axis**. As Earth orbits the Sun, sunlight hits different areas. It shines on these areas for longer periods of time. This causes seasons. Earth's four seasons are spring, summer, fall, and winter.

DID YOU KNOW?

Earth's axis tilts slightly. Why? Scientists think a large object hit Earth long ago.

axis

CHAPTER 2

LAND AND LAYERS

Earth has four layers. The crust is the outermost layer. It is the thinnest. The crust is made of solid rock. It is what we live and walk on.

crust

The top of the crust has soil.
We grow plants and **crops** in it.

soil

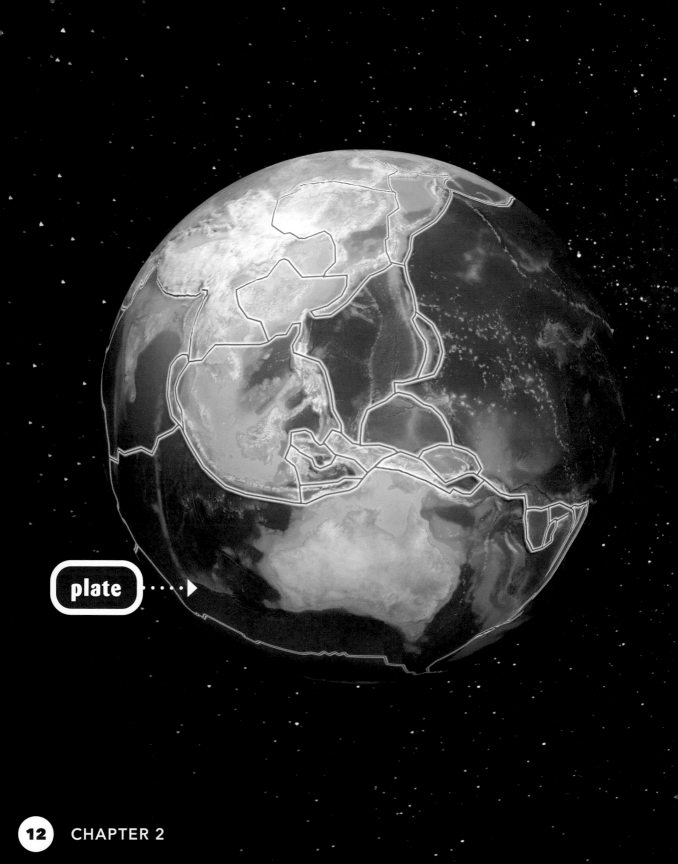

plate ·····▶

The thick layer under the crust is the mantle. The mantle is mostly solid. The crust and the upper layer of the mantle are broken up into huge pieces of rock. These pieces are called plates. They fit together like a puzzle.

Earth's plates are always moving. They move very slowly. Most move just inches each year. They move over a layer of softer, partly melted rocks in the mantle.

Plates sometimes smash together. This is how most mountains form.

Plates can move under each other. Then volcanoes can form. Hot, liquid rock called magma pushes up through Earth's crust. When a volcano erupts, hot lava flows out.

DID YOU KNOW?

Most **earthquakes** happen along cracks in the plates' edges. Plates slide and move. **Pressure** builds up and causes an earthquake.

mountain ridge

volcano

lava

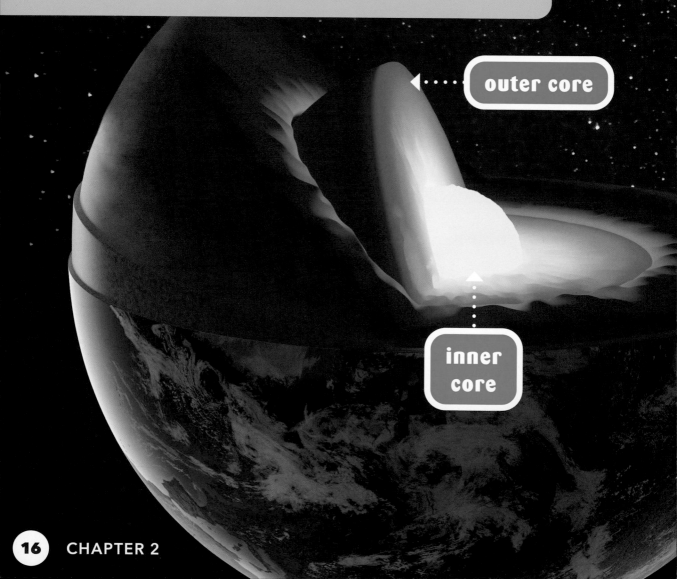

Earth's inner **core** is solid. It is made of iron and nickel. The inner core is very hot. How hot? Scientists think it could be as hot as the Sun's surface! The outer core is made of liquid iron and nickel.

outer core

inner core

TAKE A LOOK!

What are Earth's four layers? Take a look!

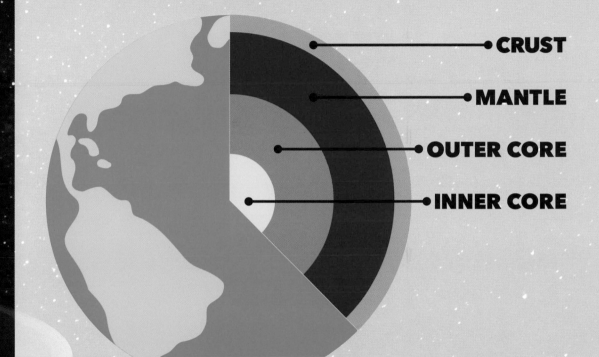

- CRUST
- MANTLE
- OUTER CORE
- INNER CORE

CHAPTER 3

THE PLANET OF LIFE

Earth is covered in a layer of gases. This is Earth's **atmosphere**. It has **oxygen**. Without it, we could not breathe. We could not survive on Earth.

atmosphere

Earth's temperatures can support life. Other planets are too hot or too cold.

Earth is our home planet. We live on its land. We breathe the oxygen in its air. We drink its water and eat the food that grows on it.

Earth is the only known planet that can support life. It has everything we need to live. What more would you like to learn about our planet?

DID YOU KNOW?

Satellites orbit Earth. They take photos. They gather information. Why? Scientists know a lot about Earth. But they want to learn more!

ACTIVITIES & TOOLS

SAVE WATER

Earth is the only planet in our solar system with liquid water on its surface. It is important that we don't waste water. Learn about how much water you use and how much you could save with this activity!

What You Need:
- large bowl
- toothbrush
- toothpaste
- liquid measuring cup

❶ The next time you brush your teeth, first place a bowl in your bathroom sink, under the faucet.

❷ Keep the faucet running slowly while you brush your teeth.

❸ After you're done brushing, turn the water off. Pour the water from the bowl into the measuring cup. How much water did you use?

❹ Pour the used water onto plants outside.

❺ The next time you brush your teeth, put the empty bowl back in the sink. Brush your teeth again. This time, only use a little bit of water when you need it.

❻ After you're done brushing, turn the water off. Pour the water from the bowl into the measuring cup. How much water did you use this time? How much water did you save when you turned the water off while brushing your teeth? What other ways can you save water?

GLOSSARY

atmosphere: The mixture of gases that surrounds a planet.

axis: An imaginary line through the center of an object, around which the object spins.

core: The center, most inner part of a planet.

crops: Plants that are grown as food.

earthquakes: Sudden, violent shakings of Earth that may damage buildings and cause injuries.

gravity: The force that pulls things toward the center of a planet or body and keeps them from floating away.

orbit: To travel in a circular path around something.

oxygen: A colorless gas found in air and water. Humans and animals need oxygen to breathe.

planet: A large body that orbits, or travels in circles around, the Sun.

pressure: The force produced by pressing on something.

satellites: Spacecraft that are sent to orbit the Sun, Moon, or planets.

solar system: The Sun, together with its orbiting bodies, such as the planets, their moons, and asteroids, comets, and meteors.

tides: The constant changes in sea level that are caused by the pull of the Moon and the Sun on Earth.

INDEX

TO LEARN MORE

Finding more information is as easy as 1, 2, 3.

❶ Go to www.factsurfer.com

❷ Enter "Earth" into the search box.

❸ Choose your book to see a list of websites.

FACT SURFER